October '98

Diana,

I hope this
book appeals to you
as it does me. It is multi-
about life, real and
dimensioned. In some ways,
your writing reminds me of Sharon's.

Enjoy. Jana Ayers

The Wellspring

The Wellspring

poems by
Sharon Olds

Alfred A. Knopf   New York   1996

THIS IS A BORZOI BOOK
PUBLISHED BY ALFRED A. KNOPF, INC.

Versions of "Bathing the New Born," "The Last Birthday at Home," "My Son the Man," and "Poem to Our Son After a High Fever" originally appeared in *The New Yorker*.

Other poems in this work were originally published in the following publications: *American Poetry Review, The Atlantic Monthly, The Beloit Poetry Journal, Elle, Field, The Iowa Review, The Nation, The New Republic, Ontario Review, Open Places, The Paris Review, Pequod, Poetry, Poetry East, Poetry Ireland Review, The Quarterly*, and *TriQuarterly*.

Library of Congress Cataloging-in-Publication Data

Olds, Sharon.
    The Wellspring / Sharon Olds.–1st ed.
        p.   cm.
    ISBN 0-679-44592-7. —ISBN 0-679-76560-3 (pbk.)
    I. Title.
    PS3565.L34W44   1996
    811'.54—dc20   95-15835
                                                      CIP

Manufactured in the United States of America
First Edition

For our daughter and son

Contents

Part 3

Part 4

Part 1

Visiting My Mother's College

This is where her body was
when it was sealed, her torso clear and whole,
she walked on these lawns. Curled as the Aesop
fox she sat in a window-seat, it
makes me sick with something like desire to think of her,
my first love—when I lay stunned
in her arms, I thought she was the whole world,
heat, smooth flesh, colostrum,
and that huge heartbeat. But here she had
no children, no husband, and her mother was dead,
no one was far weaker or far
stronger than she, she carried her rage
unknown, hidden, unknowable yet,
she moved, slowly, under the arches,
literally singing. Half of me
was deep in her body, dyed egg
with my name on it, in cursive script—
maybe the most serene time of my life, as I
glided above the gravel paths
there near the center of her universe.
I have come here to walk on the stones she walked on,
to sit in the fragrant chapel with its pews
rubbed with the taken combs of bees, its
stained, glassy God, I want to
love her when she has not hurt anyone yet,
when all that had been done to her
she held, still, in her fresh body, as she
lay on her stomach, still a child, studying
diligently for finals, and before the dance
she washed her hair and rinsed it with lemon and
shook and shook her head so the interior of her
tiny room was flecked with sour bright citrus.

My Parents' Wedding Night, 1937

Today, I thought of that blood, rippling out,
and the blood that seeps up, out of the side
of a trout when a pressed-down blade breaks through,
silvery salty sweet fish
of my mother's maidenhead. It was in the dark,
the harsh shantung blinds drawn down, the
ruffled curtains unloosed at the waist.
She was naked with a man for the first time,
the intricate embroidery silks of her
pudenda moist upright alert
terrified, thrilled, each hair
reaching out and curling back, she was
there in the bed like her own parents,
there at the center of the world. Now
she was the loaf laid into the pan
raw and being fed now into the bright oven.
And I thought of my father, over her,
ivory-white face and black hair,
up on his elbows like a man pulling himself
out of the ocean onto the beach. The war
had not yet begun, they lay and slept
in blood and peace, no one knew what was coming.

I leave them wrapped in that sheet, double larvum,
they sleep with their mouths open like teenagers
in the smell of champagne and semen and cruor,
they rest but I go back again and again to that moment,
looking at it until I get less unused to it,
like my childhood God watching Adam and Eve in the garden—
the first springing wrinkle of blood,
I see it as a castaway sees the leap
of life pouring out of the turtle's throat where the shell severs it.

The Planned Child

I hated the fact that they had planned me, she had taken
a cardboard out of his shirt from the laundry
as if sliding the backbone up out of his body,
and made a chart of the month and put
her temperature on it, rising and falling,
to know the day to make me—I would have
liked to have been conceived in heat,
in haste, by mistake, in love, in sex,
not on cardboard, the little x on the
rising line that did not fall again.

But when a friend was pouring wine
and said that I seem to have been a child who had been wanted,
I took the wine against my lips
as if my mouth were moving along
that valved wall in my mother's body, she was
bearing down, and then breathing from the mask, and then
bearing down, pressing me out into
the world that was not enough for her without me in it,
not the moon, the sun, Orion
cartwheeling across the dark, not
the earth, the sea—none of it
was enough, for her, without me.

Japanese-American Farmhouse, California, 1942

Everything has been taken that anyone
thought worth taking. The stairs are tilted,
scattered with sycamore leaves curled
like ammonites in inland rock.
Wood shows through the paint on the frame
and the door is open—an empty room,
sunlight on the floor. All that is left
on the porch is the hollow cylinder
of an Alber's Quick Oats cardboard box
and a sewing machine. Its extraterrestrial
head is bowed, its scrolled neck
glistens. I was born, that day, near there,
in wartime, of ignorant people.

Earliest Memory

Light, not bright, but deep. No beams,
light like heat, enclosed, a roomful
like a mouthful of light. And bars, upright,
which interrupt the light, stripe it
evenly: light, bar,
light solid as well water,
bar a blueish shadow, another
amber band of light, something
moving across it. Out of the narrow
doorway of a bar, and into another,
through the intervals—light,
shade, light, shade—someone
ranges slowly, freely. The bars do not
waver—vertical, identical,
they are still. The light does not dilute, it is
full, steady, within it the presence
moves, large and calm, back
and forth, back and forth, and at times,
behind and above it, for a moment, the angle of the
wall and ceiling holds, bent—
the border of the box of the world, where she swam
in light, striped, where I lay, whole, and watched.

My First Weeks

Sometimes, when I wonder what I'm like, underneath,
I think of my first two weeks, I was drenched
with happiness. The wall opened
like liquid, my head slid through, my legs, I
pushed off, from the side, soared
gently, turned, squeezed out
neatly into the cold illuminated
air and breathed it. Washed off, wrapped,
I slept, and when I woke there was the breast
the size of my head, hard and full,
the springy drupelets of the nipple. Sleep.
Milk. Heat. Every day
she held me up to the window and wagged
my fist at my sister, down in the street, who
waved her cone back at me so
hard the ice cream flew through the air like a
butter-brickle cannonball,
otherwise it was sleep and milk,
by day my mother's, by night the nurses
would prop me with a bottle. Paradise
had its laws—every four hours and not
a minute sooner I could drink, but every four
hours I could have the world in my mouth.
Two weeks, and then home, to the end of the hall,
where at night a nurse would give me four ounces of
water every four hours, and in the meantime I shrieked for it.
They knew it would build my character,
to learn to give up, and I learned it—dawn
and the satiny breast, the burp, the boiled
sheet to be placed on where my sister couldn't touch me,
I lay and moved my arms and legs like

feelers in the light. Glorious life!
And it would always be there, behind those nights
of tap water, the whole way back,
that fortnight of unlimited ration,
every four hours—clock of cream
and flame, I have known heaven.

For My Mother

You were my first child, really.
When my sister moved into the guest room
you started to come to me at night
like a child who cannot sleep, coming to
the mother's bed, so I became a mother
at seven. Like the nurse laying the firstborn
in a mother's arms, you came sometimes
and laid yourself in my arms, you were spongy and felt
almost boneless, sacs of this
and that, wet feathers across your eyes.
Where does it come from, the love of babies—
I took you in my arms without thought, I felt lucky,
your cheek to my hard, ribby chest,
its nipple flat as a stroke of color,
a spot where some god had laid a thumb
for an instant. I was not impatient, I did not
mind the boiled-egg smell you had brought
from his bed—what I wanted was to feed strength up like
heat or color into your body,
to pump life into your life. Where had I learned that?
I had learned it from you, from the months you had held me
to your breast and given me hot, plentiful
milk, it was seven years since then, I had forgotten nothing.

The Lisp

Sometimes they liked me. When I was a kid,
I lisped, I could not get my *s*'s
out without a slight spray
like the vapor in the room with the sick child,
and they liked it. My father made up a sentence
for me to say at Sunday breakfast—
Sharon swallows sausages—I would
say it and they'd laugh. They had given me my tongue,
my teeth, my lips, my life. Often,
in that house, there was required silence,
twenty-four hours of silence for a child
or silence at the table for a mother and three children, no
hand signals allowed, no American Sign Language.
And when they had me stand in the corner
there was the corner to face—shadowed right-angle
like the closed entrance to the eternal, I would stand
in silence. I would lie across her legs in silence,
as I grew bigger and bigger over the years
I began to hang over the ends of her lap
in massive shame. Christ, it was a quiet life,
but on Sundays—batter faintly seething
in the bowl, syrup from the waists of the trees,
butter off the block, and the membrane of the pig
crackling in the skillet, the knots of fat
undoing—they'd tell me to say it, mist of their
lost affection coming back on their faces,
Sharon sswallowss ssaussagess, they would
get me to say it again, they would *ask me to speak.*

Christian Child

The maroon velvet of the armrests was dense
as fur, with a nap that jumped back and forth
under my thumb. I still sucked it,
eight years old, nine, ten,
the darkness big around us, a real
theater, my mother beside me, Good Friday,
our yearly movie, three hours long,
the time that Jesus had hung on the cross,
noon to three on an April after-
noon in A.D. 33.
It began with Palm Sunday, the half-man
like a Bearded Lady coming in on the burro,
and the Last Supper, family mealtime
tainted and uneasy, and the night in the garden,
all slept but the isolated boy. Then the kiss, as if
every good thing would be taken
and turned to bad. And the pieces of silver
like the quarters in my mother's desk drawer
I took to buy doughnuts—rings, Roman
shields, swords, brushes curved forward
over the soldiers' brows. The governor
washed his hands, as if power were a stain
to come off, and the crowd chose the thief.
My mother sat rigid, the crown was like
barbed wire made into an Easter basket,
they set it on his head and tapped it into
his scalp with a cedar mallet. They made him
carry his cross through the streets, they held his
hand and spread the fingers and pressed
a blunt spike into the center of his palm
and hammered it, then the other hand, they

crossed the flattish parts of the feet
and used one nail. When he said *I thirst,*
like my brother calling for water at night, and they
raised the sponge soaked in vinegar
on the end of a stick, my mouth was open and my
eyes so open the sockets ached—I
held onto the scurf of the arm-rest
and felt my mother's body shake
with strict passion. Then they brought his mother
to the base of the cross, she looked up, up,
up, until she could see her boy.
He gave her to his friend, he turned his head and
said to the thief on the cross to his right, *This*
evening thou shalt be with me
in Paradise, I heard his voice
and some other noise, some mammal sound
coming from my mouth. *It is finished,* he said,
and then he died. I saw my pallid
hand on the velvet, horrible human
hand He had been killed for. On Sunday they would find
the stone door rolled away from the tomb,
his loin-towel perfectly folded, people would
stick the length of their finger into
the holes in him, he would walk on the lake
easily. But this was Good Friday,
San Quentin Day, my mother wiping
her small face, wild and meek.
Two more days until they hid the eggs, those
smooth dead beings the colors of flowers,
and the chocolate rabbit for the end of Lent.
I would start with the ears, solid, something to

pierce with my canines and grind my molars against, and then come to the hollow body, one bite and it exploded.

Killing My Sister's Fish

I picked up the bottle with its gladiator shoulders—
inside its shirred, greyish plastic
ammonia, more muscular than water, pungent—
I poured one dollop, gleaming genie,
into the bowl with my sister's goldfish
just because they were alive, and she liked them.
It was in the basement, near the zinc-lined sinks
and the ironing-board, next to the boiler,
beside the door to the cellar from which
I could get into the crawl space
under the corner of the house, and lie
on the dirt on my back, as if passed out.
I may have been on my way there
when I saw the bowl, and the ammonia curled
for a moment in the air like a spirit. Then I crawled up
under the floor-joists, into the tangent
where the soil curved up, and I lay there
at the ends of the earth, as if without
regret, as if something set in motion
long before I had been conceived
had been accomplished.

The Swimming Race

Noon, Orinda Park Pool, three girls
in rubber caps sculpted with rubber
roses, and they had put our fathers
at the far ends of our lanes. We curled
our toes over the edge, the gun went off—
they dove cleanly, as I jumped. By the time
I had surfaced, and started to dog-paddle, they had
finished the race, their fathers had drawn them up
dripping and were handing them sateen ribbons with
rosettes, a red and a cobalt blue,
I held up my head as he'd taught me, and swam
like a dog toward his end of the pool. The day
was temperate and cloudless, live-oaks
in a sharp cluster full of yellow-jackets to my left,
the lawn to my right, and there before me,
at the end of my lane—black lines
on the bottom of the pool, where the drowned would lie—
was my father. I paddled, I felt myself approach him,
I was grinning because of the prize I would win
for coming in third, a Big Hunk bar—
the milk and honey on the other side—
and because my father was getting bigger,
leaning toward me, his arms open.
He pulled me out, and held my hand
up by the wrist. My sister sneered, she said
Why did you lift Shary's fist
when she was last? and he smiled, a smile almost
without meanness, one of the last
times we saw him smile, he said
I thought she was the winner of the next race, and his
face flushed with pleasure and the shade of the yardarm.

Parents' Day

I breathed shallow as I looked for her
in the crowd of oncoming parents, I strained
forward, like a gazehound held back on a leash,
then I raced toward her. I remember her being
much bigger than I, her smile of the highest
wattage, a little stiff, sparkling
with consciousness of her prettiness—I
pitied the other girls for having mothers
who looked like mothers, who did not blush.
Sometimes she would have braids around her head like a
goddess or an advertisement for California raisins—
I worshipped her cleanliness, her transfixing
irises, sometimes I thought she could
sense a few genes of hers
dotted here and there in my body
like bits of undissolved sugar
in a recipe that did not quite work out.
For years, when I thought of her, I thought
of the long souring of her life, but on Parents' Day
my heart would bang and my lungs swell so I could
feel the tucks and puckers of embroidered
smocking on my chest press into my ribs,
my washboard front vibrate like scraped
tin to see that woman arriving
and to know she was mine.

Dirty Memories

The boy down the street dug a pit, in his yard,
four feet deep, and watered it,
and asked us girls, one by one,
to come over and play, to stand on the edge
and close our eyes, and he pushed us into
the pit. The mud was glossy, he seemed
hardly to notice us, he just
wanted to push another one in.
And someone dared the girl up the street
to touch a piece of dog-do on the sidewalk,
and when she picked it up he dared her
to eat it, I can see the soft disc of it
on the edge of her new front tooth. We climbed
the pig-iron gates at the foot of the street,
gates which we did not know marked
a border of a neighborhood
signed over, in secret, to Christians, who were white,
and Anglo-Saxon, and Protestant,
we threw pebbles at college boys in convertibles
and ran through a windowless garage over
a studded, steel turntable,
my calves weak and hot with excitement.
And heat spread in my chest in fifth grade when I
offered orange juice to that child in the lunchroom,
then told him there wasn't any—Do you want
orange juice? Well, there isn't any—
to see his face small as my brother's
crumple, like the thinnest paper
cup. I'm talking about the power of putting

poison into the bowl with my sister's
fish. My chest was hot as I poured,
I'm saying I was *glad*.

Mrs. Krikorian

She saved me. When I arrived in sixth grade,
a known criminal, the new teacher
asked me to stay after school the first day, she said
I've heard about you. She was a tall woman,
with a deep crevice between her breasts,
and a large, calm nose. She said,
This is a special library pass.
As soon as you finish your hour's work—
that hour's work that took ten minutes
and then the devil glanced into the room
and found me empty, a house standing open—
you can go to the library. Every hour
I'd zip through the work, and slip out of
my seat as if out of God's side and sail
down to the library, down through the empty
powerful halls, flash my pass
and stroll over to the dictionary
to look up the most interesting word
I knew, *spank*, dipping two fingers
into the jar of library paste to
suck that tart mucilage as I
came to the page with the cocker spaniel's
silks curling up like the fine steam of the body.
After *spank*, and *breast*, I'd move on
to *Abe Lincoln* and *Helen Keller*,
safe in their goodness till the bell, thanks
to Mrs. Krikorian, amiable giantess
with the kind eyes. When she asked me to write
a play, and direct it, and it was a flop,
and I hid in the coat-closet, she brought me a candy-cane
as you lay a peppermint on the tongue, and the worm

will come up out of the bowel to get it.
And so I was emptied of Lucifer
and filled with school glue and eros and
Amelia Earhart, saved by Mrs. Krikorian.
And who had saved Mrs. Krikorian?
When the Turks came across Armenia,
who slid her into the belly of a quilt, who
locked her in a chest, who mailed her to America?
And *that* one, who saved *her*, and *that* one—
who saved *her*, to save the one
who saved Mrs. Krikorian, who was
standing there on the sill of sixth grade, a
wide-hipped angel, smokey hair
standing up lightly all around her head?
I end up owing my soul to so many,
to the Armenian nation, one more soul someone
jammed behind a stove, drove
deep into a crack in a wall,
shoved under a bed. I would wake
up, in the morning, under my bed—not
knowing how I had got there—and lie
in the dusk, the dustballs beside my face
round and ashen, shining slightly
with the eerie comfort of what is neither good nor evil.

Part 2

Necking

I remember the Arabic numerals on the dashboards,
aquarium green, like the paintbrush tips
the watch-girls licked, licking the radium—
we were there above the Cyclotron,
in the hills, the Rad Lab under us
enclosed in its cyclone fence. The interiors
of the cars were shaped like soft flanks,
the cloth front seats plump as some mothers'
laps. I remember the beauty of the night,
the crisp weightless blackness, the air
that rose up the slope straight from the sea,
from Seal Rock—we slid slowly
along each other. Berkeley, below,
without my glasses, was like a bottom
drawer of smeared light. The rape
and murder of our classmate had happened in these hills,
so the fragrance of the dirt, porous and mineral,
—eucalyptus and redwood humus—
that had buried her body, was there with sex,
and one gleam down there was the doughnut shop
where he had picked her up—as if the intimate
pleasure of eating doughnuts, now,
for all of us, were to bear his mark.
And the easy touch of the four thousand volts,
that was in the car with us
with everything else—the rivets in boys' jeans,
their soldered clothes, the way they carried
the longing of the species, you could not help but pity them
as they set you on stunned fire. I would almost
pass out, my body made of some other
substance, my eyes open in the green darkness

of some other planet. And in some other
car, on some other skirt of the mountain,
a boy I secretly adored. I remember
how it felt, eyes closed, kissing,
streaming through the night, sealed in a capsule
with the wrong person. But the place was right,
mountains on my left hand,
sea on my right, I felt someday I might find him,
proton electron we would hit and stick and
meanwhile there were the stars, and the careful not
looking at or touching the boy's pants,
and my glasses, wings folded, stuck
in a pocket. I can hear the loud snap
when we leaned on them and they broke, we drove down the
hill, the porch-lamp blazed, I would enter
below its blurred gem, it seemed
endless then, the apprenticeship to the mortal.

First

He stood in the sulphur baths, his calves
against the stone rim of the pool
where his half-full glass of scotch stood, his
shins wavering in the water, his torso
looming over me, huge, in the night,
a grown-up man's body, softer and
warmer with the clothes off—I was a sophomore
at college, in the baths with a naked man,
a writer, married, a father, widowed,
remarried, separated, unreadable, and when I
said No, I was sorry, I couldn't,
he had invented this, rising and dripping
in the heavy sodium water, giving me
his body to suck. I had not heard
of this, I was moved by his innocence and daring,
I went to him like a baby who's been crying
for hours for milk. He stood and moaned
and rocked his knees, I felt I knew
what his body wanted me to do, like rubbing
my mother's back, receiving directions
from her want into the nerves of my hands.
In the smell of the trees of seaweed rooted in
ocean trenches just offshore,
and the mineral liquid from inside the mountain,
I gave over to flesh like church music
until he drew out and held himself and
something flew past me like a fresh ghost.
We sank into the water, and lay there, napes
on the rim. *I've never done that before,*
I said. His eyes not visible
to me, his voice muffled, he said, *You've been*

sucking cock since you were fourteen,
and fell asleep. I stayed beside him
so he wouldn't go under, he snored like my father, I
tried not to think about what he had said,
but then I saw, in it, the unmeant
gift—that I was good at this
raw mystery I liked. I sat
and rocked, by myself, in the fog, in the smell
of kelp, the night steam like animals' breath,
there where the harsh granite and quartz dropped down
into and under the start of the western sea.

Adolescence

When I think of my adolescence, I think
of the bathroom of that seedy hotel
in San Francisco, where my boyfriend would take me.
I had never seen a bathroom like that—
no curtains, no towels, no mirror, just
a sink green with grime and a toilet
yellow and rust-colored—like something in a science experiment,
growing the plague in bowls.
Sex was still a crime, then,
I'd sign out of my college dorm
to a false destination, sign into
the flophouse under a false name,
go down the hall to the one bathroom
and lock myself in. And I could not learn to get that
diaphragm in, I'd decorate it
like a cake, with glistening spermicide,
and lean over, and it would leap from my fingers
and sail into a corner, to land
in a concave depression like a rat's nest,
I'd bend and pluck it out and wash it
and wash it down to that fragile dome,
I'd frost it again till it was shimmering
and bend it into its little arc and it would
fly through the air, rim humming
like Saturn's ring, I would bow down and crawl to retrieve it.
When I think of being eighteen
that's what I see, that brimmed disc
floating through the air and descending, I see myself
kneeling, reaching for my life.

Early Images of Heaven

It amazed me that the shapes of penises,
their sizes, and angles, everything about them
was the way I would have designed them if I had
invented them. The skin, the way the skin
thickens and thins, its suppleness,
the way the head barely fits in the throat,
its mouth almost touching the valve of the stomach—
and the hair, which lifts, or crinkles, delicate
and free—I could not get over all this,
the passion for it as intense in me
as if it were made to my order, or my
desire made to its order—as if I had
known it before I was born, as if
I remembered coming through it, like God
the Father all around me.

Celibacy at Twenty

After I broke up with someone,
or someone with me, days would go by,
nights, weeks, soon it would be months since I had
touched anyone. I would move as little
as possible, the air seemed to press on my skin, my
breasts like something broken open, un-
capped and not covered, the buds floated in the
center at the front, if I turned a corner too
fast I would almost come. Swollen,
walking like someone carrying something
filled to the brim, the lip of the liquid
rocking, taut, at the edge, at the top—
and at times, in the shower, no matter how quickly
I washed I'd be over the top in seconds,
and then the loneliness, which had felt enormous,
would begin to grow, easily, rapidly,
triple, sextuple, dodecatuple,
the palm fronds and camellia buds bent
double under a campus sky of iron.
Later, when the next first kiss would come,
it would shock me, the size and power of happiness,
and yet it was familiar—lips aching and
pulling, hands and feet going numb, I'd be
trying not to moan, streaming slowly
across the arc of the sky—it was always
a return, the face in the dashlight closer
and closer, like the approaching earth,
until it is all you can see. Each time,
I wanted to be coming home
to stay. But every time I went
from months of hunger to those first kisses,

soon there were the last kisses, and I
felt I stood outside of life, held
back—but no one was holding me, I was
waiting, very near the human,
my violence uncommitted, I was
saving it. Once I stripped and
entered the pit I did not want ever to come up out of it.

The Source

It became the deep spring of my life,
I didn't know if it was a sickness or a gift.
To reach around both sides of a man,
one palm to one buttock,
the other palm to the other, the way we are split,
to grasp that band of muscle on the male
haunch and help guide the massed
heavy nerve down my throat until it
stoppers the hole behind the breastbone that is always hungry,
then I feel complete. To be lifted
onto a man—the male breast
so hard, there seem no chambers in it, it is
lifting-muscle—and set tight as a lock-slot down
onto a bolt, we are looking into
each other's eyes as if the matter of the iris were
a membrane deep in the body dissolving now,
it is what I had dreamed, to meet men
fully, as a woman twin, unborn,
half-gelled, clasped, nothing between us
but our bodies, naked, and when those dissolve,
nothing between us—or perhaps I vanish
and the man is still there, as if I have been trying
to disappear, into them,
to be myself the glass of sourmash
my father lifted to his mouth. Ah, I am in him,
I slide all the way down to the beginning, the
curved chamber of the balls. My brothers
and sisters are there, swimming by the cinerous
millions, I say to them, Stay here—
for the children of this father it may be the better life;
but they cannot hear. Blind, deaf,

armless, brainless, they plunge forward,
driven, desperate to enter the other, to
die in her, and wake. For a moment,
after we wake, we are without desire—
five, ten, twenty seconds of
pure calm, as if each one of us is whole.

Making Love

You wake up, and you do not know
where you are, or who you are
or what you are, the last light of the evening
coming up to the panes, not coming in,
the solid, slanted body of the desk
between the windows, its bird's-eye slightly
shining, here and there, in the wood. And you
try to think back, you cannot remember it,
it stands behind your mind, like a mountain,
at night, behind you, your pants are torn
or across the room or still dangling from one leg
like a heavy scarlet loop of the body, your
bra is half on or not on or you were naked to begin with,
you cannot remember, everything is changed.
Tomorrow, maybe, taking a child to school,
your foot in the air half off the curb you'll
see his mouth where it was and feel it and the
large double star of your two bodies,
but for now you are like the one in the crib,
you are everyone, right now,
the milky, greenish windows still as
sentinels, saying, *Don't worry,*
you will not remember, you will never know.

I Love It When

I love it when you roll over
and lie on me in the night, your weight
steady on me as tons of water, my
lungs like a little, shut box,
the firm, haired surface of your legs
opening my legs, my heart swells
to a taut purple boxing glove and then
sometimes I love to lie there doing
nothing, my powerful arms thrown down,
bolts of muslin rippling from the selvage,
your pubic bone a pyramid set
point down on the point of another
—glistening fulcrum. Then, in the stillness,
I love to feel you grow and grow be-
tween my legs like a plant in fast motion
the way, in the auditorium, in the
dark, near the beginning of our lives,
above us, the enormous stems and flowers
unfolded in silence.

The Dragons

Something moves on the grass, bent
as if broken and badly mended, twists
and jerks on the scorched lawn, at noon—
in the lens of my binoculars,
the copulators. I almost feel I could
know how she feels with her barbed forearms
cocked and scrabbling for a hold, his tail-point
torqued and locked to hers. Like one wrecked
being they topple, like a tiny ball of Scotch
tape and gauze they fry. I cannot
tell if she's trying to escape, or to twist
closer, they fall and writhe like something
in a fire—turned now in profile they ramp
like an ancient Egyptian brother and sister
in single bristling file, then,
suddenly, he drops, like someone shot dead,
they lie a moment undoing themselves
and then he's gone—flown off—I do not
think they will find each other again.
She stands there a moment, like a dry newborn
calf shaky on her legs, head down,
wings blazing in the glare, and then
she is not there, somewhere in the heat
she flies, the interior of her ovichamber
swimming like an inland sea.

After Making Love in Winter

At first, not even a sheet on me,
anything at all is painful, a plate of
lead laid down on the nerves, I lie there
and slowly I cool off—hot,
warm, cool, cold, icy, till the
skin all over my body is ice
except at the places where our flesh touches
like tiny bonfires. Between the door
and its frame, and between the transom and its frame,
the hall-light burns in straight lines
which cast up beams on the ceiling like a headless
figure flinging up her arms for joy.
In the mirror, the angles of our room seem calm,
it is the hour when we can see that the angle itself is blessed,
I gaze, in the mirror, at the smokey bulbs
of the chandelier, I feel I could be
looking at my ovaries, it is
clear that everything I see is real
and good. We have come to the end of questions,
you move your palm along my face
over and over, over and over, as if
putting the finishing touches on, before
sending me down to be born. But I don't
want to be born, I want to stay here
with you.

May 1968

When the Dean said we could not cross campus
until the students gave up the buildings,
we lay down, in the street,
we said the cops will enter this gate
over us. Lying back on the cobbles,
I saw the buildings of New York City
from dirt level, they soared up
and stopped, chopped off—above them, the sky,
the night air over the island.
The mounted police moved, near us,
while we sang, and then I began to count,
12, 13, 14, 15,
I counted again, 15, 16, one
month since the day on that deserted beach,
17, 18, my mouth fell open,
my hair on the street,
if my period did not come tonight
I was pregnant. I could see the sole of a cop's
shoe, the gelding's belly, its genitals—
if they took me to Women's Detention and did
the exam on me, the speculum,
the fingers—I gazed into the horse's tail
like a comet-train. All week, I had
thought about getting arrested, half-longed
to give myself away. On the tar—
one brain in my head, another,
in the making, near the base of my tail—
I looked at the steel arc of the horse's
shoe, the curve of its belly, the cop's
nightstick, the buildings streaming up
away from the earth. I knew I should get up

and leave, but I lay there looking at the space
above us, until it turned deep blue and then
ashy, colorless, *Give me this one*
night, I thought, *and I'll give this child*
the rest of my life, the horses' heads,
this time, drooping, dipping, until
they slept in a circle around my body and my daughter.

Part 3

First Birth

I had thought so little, really, of *her*,
inside me, all that time, not breathing—
intelligent, maybe curious,
her eyes closed. When the vagina opened,
slowly, from within, from the top, my eyes
rounded in shock and awe, it was like being
entered for the first time, but entered
from the inside, the child coming in
from the other world. Enormous, stately,
she was pressed through the channel, she turned, and rose,
they held her up by a very small ankle,
she dangled indigo and scarlet, and spread
her arms out in this world. Each thing
I did, then, I did for the first
time, touched the flesh of our flesh,
brought the tiny mouth to my breast,
she drew the avalanche of milk
down off the mountain, I felt as if
I was nothing, no one, I was everything to her, I was hers.

Her First Week

She was so small I would scan the crib a half-second
to find her, face-down in a corner, limp
as something gently flung down, or fallen
from some sky an inch above the mattress. I would
tuck her arm along her side
and slowly turn her over. She would tumble
over part by part, like a load
of damp laundry, in the dryer, I'd slip
a hand in, under her neck,
slide the other under her back,
and evenly lift her up. Her little bottom
sat in my palm, her chest contained
the puckered, moire sacs, and her neck—
I was afraid of her neck, once I almost
thought I heard it quietly snap,
I looked at her and she swivelled her slate
eyes and looked at me. It was in
my care, the creature of her spine, like the first
chordate, as if the history
of the vertebrate had been placed in my hands.
Every time I checked, she was still
with us—someday, there would be a human
race. I could not see it in her eyes,
but when I fed her, gathered her
like a loose bouquet to my side and offered
the breast, greyish-white, and struck with
minuscule scars like creeks in sunlight, I
felt she was serious, I believed she was willing to stay.

Bathing the New Born

I love with an almost fearful love
to remember the first baths I gave him—
our second child, our first son—
I laid the little torso along
my left forearm, nape of the neck
in the crook of my elbow, hips nearly as
small as a least tern's hips
against my wrist, thigh held loosely
in the loop of thumb and forefinger, the
sign that means exactly right. I'd soap him,
the long, violet, cold feet,
the scrotum wrinkled as a waved whelk shell
so new it was flexible yet, the chest,
the hands, the clavicles, the throat, the gummy
furze of the scalp. When I got him too soapy he'd
slide in my grip like an armful of buttered
noodles, but I'd hold him not too tight,
I felt that I was good for him,
I'd tell him about his wonderful body
and the wonderful soap, and he'd look up at me,
one week old, his eyes still wide
and apprehensive. I love that time
when you croon and croon to them, you can see
the calm slowly entering them, you can
sense it in your clasping hand,
the little spine relaxing against
the muscle of your forearm, you feel the fear
leaving their bodies, he lay in the blue
oval plastic baby tub and
looked at me in wonder and began to
move his silky limbs at will in the water.

History of Medicine

Finally I fondly remember even Benylin,
Robitussin, Actifed,
Tedral, erythromycin,
penicillin, E.E.S., I can
see the tidy open mouth
and the spoon's regular journey toward it,
the bowl almost convex with its shuddering
load of blackish maroon.
Time slowed down as the spoon went in, I can
still feel the thrum, in the handle,
that little tug like nursing, and then
the pulling of the spoon out of the mouth,
ampicillin, ipecac, St.
Joseph's, tetracycline, my body
tuned to the four-hour intervals—we made
one being, the bottle and the child and I,
I remember it with longing. Even the ear-drops,
lice-shampoo, wart-glaze,
even the time when our son would not take
his Tedral, he was standing in his crib
and he spat it out and I gently jammed another
dose through his teeth and he spat it out
until the bars and cruising rail
were splattered with dots of heavy syrup and he
understood I cared about the matter
even more than he.
As I cleaned him up with a damp cloth
I told him the germs were strong, we had to
staunchly fight them—I can hear my voice,

calm and cheerful. I can see myself,
a young woman with an orderly array of
bottles behind her, she is struggling to be good, to be healed.

Milk-Bubble Ruins

In the long, indolent mornings of fifth-grade
spring vacation, our son sits with the
tag-ends of his breakfast, and blows bubbles in his milk
with a blue straw, and I sit and watch him.
The foam rises furiously
in a dome over the rim of his cup,
we gaze into the edifice of fluid,
its multiple chambers. He puffs and they pile up,
they burst, they subside, he breathes out slowly, and the
multicellular clouds rise,
he inserts the straw into a single globe
and blows a little, and it swells. Ten years ago
he lay along my arm, drinking.
Now, in late March, he shows me
the white light
pop and dissolve as he
conjures and breaks each small room of milk.

Socks

I'll play Ninja Death with you
tonight, if you buy new socks, I say
to our son. After supper he holds out his foot,
the sock with a hole for its heel, I whisk it
into the wastebasket. He is tired, allergic,
his hands full of Ninja Death leaflets,
I take a sock from the bag, heft his
Achilles tendon in my palm and pull the
cotton over the arch and instep,
I have not done this for years, I feel
intensely happy, drawing the sock
up the calf—*Other foot*—
as if we are back in the days of my great
usefulness. We cast the dice
for how we will fight, I *swing* my *mace*,
he *ducks, parries* with his *chain*, I'm *dazed*, then
stunned. Day after day, year after
year I dressed our little beloveds
as if it were a life's work,
stretching the necks of the shirts to get them
over their heads, guarding the nape as I
swooped them on their back to slide overalls on—
back through the toddler clothes to the one-year
clothes to those gauzy infant-suits that un-
snapped along each seam to lie
fully open, like the body first offered to the
soul to clothe it, the mother given to the child.

A Mother at the End of June

After they go away to summer camp
I'm alone in the house in the early evening,
watching a twi-night double-header,
lilt of the pallid uniforms,
a pitch loops in, like a milk snake toward a mouse,
and behind the batter, in the front row,
a little oval sphere starts to grow
like a ball of night, coming toward me,
I glimpse it and feel like crying—oh,
it's a yawn, on a very young girl, her mouth
the shape of the well of a catcher's mitt.
How many shut-eyed cat-like yawns,
or yawns spilling milk out of the corner
like a ball tipping out of an outfielder's glove,
or huge yawns, inner deeps
of the throat showing, have opened their black
morning glories in this house? Little mouth, I looked
down into you and saw a hunger
I thought I could slake, but I could only slake and feed.

Twelve Years Old

When our daughter and her friend walk away
at the swimming pool, I see her friend's
stick legs, thin as legs
drawn by a child, and I suddenly notice
that our child's hips and thighs have swelled
so they taper to the knee. And her flesh is more liquid
than it was. The femur in her pelvic socket
orbits in a more elliptical way,
her joints gently rocking her body
as she walks toward the diving board, the front of her
torso smooth, symmetrical,
but her buttocks begin to flash their signals,
Soon, now. She climbs the ladder,
the skin all over her body twinkles,
she walks with a mild sway down the board which
shudders like a dowser's rod, the water
below her crowded with college boys, she
grins at me, her head sleek, she
decants herself out and down, her body
plummets through the air in silence and then
enters the water with the charged thrust of her
knife into the chicken in a dream when she is really hungry.

The Hand

After he falls, and his elbow is turned backwards,
our son's hand wastes away,
and we learn to know this left hand
as it is now, muscles atrophied,
fingers decurved. I try not to envision it
healed, it seems somehow disloyal;
I consider careers he can have with one-and-a-
half hands. When the doctor has stuck
the needles into his forearm and unloosed
the current, there is a crackling on the monitor,
a scribble of activity on the screen, my throat
thickens as I hear the life of the nerve,
and the doctor says, A healthy nerve
doesn't sound like this at all,
this nerve is dead. For a second I had pictured
the muscle at the base of his thumb, *flexor*
pollicis brevis, and the heel of his hand,
risen again, like dough under
a doubling-cloth. Years later,
I saw him in the album, holding his weak hand
in his strong one, the way he used to hold it,
as if carrying a sleeping marmoset,
it was eighteen months after the accident,
we did not know if the hand would come back or not—
that was the way we talked, then,
as if the hand were on a journey,
we chatted about the dead nerve,
the tendon transplant they'd try later
if the hand did not come back. All year he seemed happy,
a boy with one hand curled up
like a day-old day lily. What did he think of

at night? He had no God, he had
himself, a hand like a mouse to take care of,
the way he took care of Cowboy and Tiger,
cozying them against his clavicle.
He had what the day had brought him—as when he was
a newborn he never cried, my mother
wondered if he was all right, the way he always smiled.
Even before he was fully born, when he
looked around him, he seemed content,
I saw him in the little birth-room mirror,
his bluish head turning, his shoulders and
body inside my body, as if in this
new life, from the neck down
you wore your mother.
His eyes seemed even then to focus,
as if he knew this place, or had not
expected to know it.

Good Will

Sorting clothes, I find our son's old
jeans, the dirt worn so deeply in
they are almost tan, worked as a palimpsest,
the nub down to a flat gloss,
the metal of the rivets soured to ochre,
the back pockets curved like shields,
their stitching is like water far from land,
a long continuous swell. *Lee,*
the pants say in auric print,
LEE, they say in letters branded
in leather on the waistband, like the voice of a boy's
pants, the snap's rattle, the rough
descending and ascending scale of the zipper,
the coin-slot pocket inside the front pocket.
He had waited inside me so many years, his
egg in my side before I was born,
and he sprang fresh in his father that morning,
I had seen it long ago in science,
I shake out the jeans, and there are the knees
exploded, the white threads hanging
outside the body, the frail, torn,
blue knee open, singing of the boy.

Lament

Finally someone knocks it over and breaks it
like a mercy killing, the cow butter dish,
it cracks neatly into five pieces,
opening like an earthenware flower on the floor,
a crescent of terracotta, a dry
bisque side, a rogue shard,
the cow herself broken free, hollow,
the oval hole of the throat leading into
the cul-de-sac inside her head.
Long, drawn-out ending of my motherhood,
these two who are home less and less—
better to smash some china like the end
of a love-affair. I take her in my hand,
convex flanks fitting my palm,
thumb and forefinger holding her neck at the
carotids, kiss her mild
dumb forehead, and look into her empty
body smooth and contoured in curves
like the sexual chamber inside a woman—
the way God might have sat on the bank
shaping the clay.
Even on the hottest day, if you
soaked her in cold water in the morning
and set her on the dish, she would keep the butter
cool till night in the cavern of her body,
fresh, and pliant.

Poem to Our Son After a High Fever

When what you hear speeds up, again,
and gets too loud, and I call the doctor,
and I'm waiting for her to call back,
I think of the skin of your throat, greenish
as the ice at the edge of the pond when it starts to melt,
and the back of your neck, sometimes mottled as the
moss found on the north sides of trees.
I think of the insides of your wrists, their
dusty ivory waxy glow like
saints' candles fallen in the detritus
behind the altar, where the mice live
and propagate, feeding their young on the
crumbs of the Host like little rough pieces of light,
I think about the faint layer of grime all over your body
as if you'd been dredged with the soil of the earth
like a sacred object, and how light catches on each
facet of grit so you gleamed with a rubbed
haze. They held you as you came forth from me
in slow pulses, one, two, three—
head, shoulders, all—your feet like the
flukes of a tail as they lifted you up,
flecked with random blood bits,
like a child freckled with crumbs after a long journey,
fallen asleep next to a train window,
the fields of ice going by in the evening,
the way your brain falls asleep a few times a day now for a few minutes
and everything seems to be going fast and loud.
I picture your brain, like a blue-grey cauliflower,
the leaves, with their veins, wrapped around the stem and the heart,
I think of your navel, small rose
always folded, I think of your penis, its

candor and virtue, I picture your long
narrow feet and your bony chest and your
clever hands, you let them lie in your lap
when the episode comes, you wait for it to be over.
I think of every part of your body,
thought being a form of prayer,
but it's hard to think of your face, the globe
forehead, the speckled cheeks, the mouth
tensed, and the eyes—I can hardly stand
to see the courage there, the calmness of the
fear, as if you are prepared to bear
anything.

Prayer During That Time

I would sometimes find myself leaning on a doorframe,
a woman without belief, praying:
Please don't let anything happen to him.
Don't take his thoughts away,
don't go up to his small, dazzled
brain on the high wire and push it off.
Don't leave him drooling in his cereal. And yet
if that's the only way we can have him
please let us have him—
even if all we can see in his face
are the avenues, empty and spacious—
and put a bib on him again,
and spoon him brown sugar, and hominy,
and sit with him for the rest of our days,
wanting to keep him here even though
he might be in hell. But alive! But alive in *hell*.

Forty-One, Alone, No Gerbil

In the strange quiet, I realize
there's no one else in the house. No bucktooth
mouth pulls at a stainless-steel teat, no
hairy mammal runs on a treadmill—
Charlie is dead, the last of our children's half-children.
When our daughter found him lying in the shavings, trans-
mogrified backwards from a living body
into a bolt of rodent bread
she turned her back on early motherhood
and went on single, with nothing. Crackers,
Fluffy, Pretzel, Biscuit, Charlie,
buried on the old farm we bought
where she could know nature. Well, now she knows it
and it sucks. Creatures she loved, mobile and
needy, have gone down stiff and indifferent,
she will not adopt again though she cannot
have children yet, her body like a blueprint
of the understructure for a woman's body,
so now everything stops for a while,
now I must wait many years
to hear in this house again the faint
powerful call of a young animal.

The Cast

When the doctor cut off our son's cast
the scream of the saw filled the room
and our boy's lap was covered with fluff
like down in a hen-yard. Down the seam
that runs alongside the outside of the arm
and up the seam along the inside—that
line where the color of his white arm
changes like a brook-trout from lacteal to prismatic,
the saw moved cleanly—the saw that does not cut flesh,
the doctor told us, smiling. Then
its shrieking ran down four octaves to nothing
and the doctor took a chrome wedge
like a church key, and jimmied at the cracks
until, with a creak, the glossy false arm
opened, and there lay our son's smudged
forearm, thin as a sapling branch.
He lifted it high, in astonishment,
It's so light! Light was coming out of his eyes,
he stroked the cast with his fingertips
like a caress, and smiled, and picked up
the halves and fit them together, and gripped it
and carried it out through the waiting room
and everyone smiled, the way we smile
at a wedding, when we see the two who have been joined.

The Siblings

When our daughter's cough brings on choking attacks,
our son looks at his big sister
speculatively. When the laryngismus
begins in the kitchen, he tilts his head
and asks, *Is she taking her little pills?*, this
boy who has swallowed horse-pills for years.
She hacks, she gags, she chokes, the physical
tears come out of her eyes, and her brother
seems to wonder—is the girl mortal,
the girl with the math scores, the faultless speller,
his critic, who has never cut herself
or spilled her milk? From out of his life
a little too rich with injury and illness
he ponders this female paragon,
and can hear, around the corner, her quiet
crying when the doctor takes her blood, he
glances at the mesh of his bandage, as if
he feels relief he drew the short
straw of his own life. When she comes
out, suffused with sorrow and sincerity
and intransigence, her face blotched
with sullen grief, he takes her by the hand and says
Let's go get baby sister a treat,
he leads her over to the elevator, he
presses Down, he will accompany her down into life.

Love's Eyesight

When we drive away after Visitor's Day,
first I see him whole, smiling slightly
and waving, then I see only his arm
through a scrim of leaves, and then I am not
sure I see him, a shaded hand
behind a spray of pine-needles, his
hair next to some dust-brown bark—
the car pulls away until no atom
of what I am seeing behind us is our son, and a
mile down the camp road I have forgotten
the pattern of the freckles on his face, the exact
shade of the blue of his eyes, as if I have
lost him. When he first came into being
in me, he did not look human, then slowly
he formed, a head, a body, the boy
unfolding, limbs springing free and uncurling—
with a clear tap he kicked me from within—
long before I saw his face
I felt I knew him, I could not have described him and I loved him.

The Transformed Boy

At twelve, he stops wearing polo shirts,
those dirt-softened dust-cloths, he stops leaving
his hair uncombed. At camp, they were all
animals, he says—his camp
girlfriend would see his naked knees
every day, but when our son
has his first school girlfriend,
suddenly he is brushing his teeth,
and parting his hair like the map of Kansas,
combing one wheat field this way
and one field that. The oval, long
shape of his head suddenly shows,
he takes to wearing oxford shirts,
he spends an hour at the dressing-room mirror
checking his hair, studying a shirt, its
sleeves a little big, yet,
the fresh broadcloth wrinkling softly
like long-in-bathwater skin, the cuffs
loosely clasping his narrow wrists with
dignity. Now he is ready
to take her arm and lead her into the mirror.
You think that boys have all the power,
he says, but it's the girls who let you
know if the one you like will say yes,
and then, if you're lucky, you ask her.

The Last Birthday at Home

The last night before you were born, you were
almost complete, your mind busy,
without language, but full of motion
which would never be remembered or know itself.
The last night that you did not exist,
nine months before that—
from here it looks almost impossible,
our path to you and not one of the others.
If we had to go back and find you again,
like families looking for each other after war—
it frightens me how close we came
to missing you. If we had not walked down that
beach, if that side of the island had not been
deserted . . . Like a violent, delicate job of
rescue we got you out. Again we're in the
month of Saturn, its rings coiled loose around its
body, glittering discs of dust which we would
step through if we gave our weight to them, we
walked across them and stood at the moment of your appearing.

Solo

Our son shrugs into his macho jacket
with the swollen shoulders, he swings his sports bag
over his shoulder, runs his fingers through his
blown-dry feather-cut, raises an eyebrow,
tosses his keys, flips a token and is
out the door to karate—in the bag
his *gi* and belt lie coiled.
I turn the lock, I lean on the door
and hear him joggle the old elevator button and then
kick it with a flying kick,
and then I hear it, for the first time,
and the last time, I hear him sing
five or six pure, slow
soprano notes, like part of a Mass,
Mass for the end of a man's childhood.
Just those few, clear tones
in the hall narrow as an echo chamber,
A, B♭, C, F,
whole, isolated, sweet, that voice
which has not changed since it first sounded,
his throat opens, and he breathes a low O.

Physics

Her first puzzle had three pieces,
she'd take the last piece, and turn it,
and lower it in, like a sewer-lid,
flush with the street. The bases of the frames
were like wooden fur, guard-hairs sticking out of the
pelt. I'd set one on the floor and spread
the pieces out around it. It makes me
groan to think of Red Riding Hood's hood
a single, scarlet, pointed piece, how
long since I have seen her. Later, panthers,
500 pieces, and an Annunciation,
1000 pieces, we would gaze, on our elbows,
into its gaps. Now she tells me
that if I were sitting in a twenty-foot barn,
with the doors open at either end,
and a fifty-foot ladder hurtled through the barn
at the speed of light, there would be a moment
—after the last rung was inside the barn
and before the first rung came out the other end—
when the whole fifty-foot ladder would be
inside the twenty-foot barn, and I believe her,
I have thought her life was inside my life
like that. When she reads the college catalogues, I
look away and hum. I have not grown up
yet, I have lived as my daughter's mother
the way I had lived as my mother's daughter,
inside her life. I have not been born yet.

My Son the Man

Suddenly his shoulders get a lot wider,
the way Houdini would expand his body
while people were putting him in chains. It seems
no time since I would help him to put on his sleeper,
guide his calves into the gold interior,
zip him up and toss him up and
catch his weight. I cannot imagine him
no longer a child, and I know I must get ready,
get over my fear of men now my son
is going to be one. This was not
what I had in mind when he pressed up through me like a
sealed trunk through the ice of the Hudson,
snapped the padlock, unsnaked the chains,
and appeared in my arms. Now he looks at me
the way Houdini studied a box
to learn the way out, then smiled and let himself be manacled.

First Formal

She rises up above the strapless, her dewy
flesh like a soul half out of a body.
It makes me remember her one week old,
soft, elegant, startled, alone.
She stands still, as if, if she moved,
her body might pour up out of the bodice,
she keeps her steady gaze raised
when she walks, she looks exactly forward,
led by some radar of the strapless, or with
a cup runneth over held perfectly level, her
almost sea-sick beauty shimmering
a little. She looks brave, shoulders
made of some extra-visible element,
or as if some of her cells, tonight,
were faceted like a fly's eye, and her
skin was seeing us see it. She looks
hatched this moment, and yet weary—she would lie
in her crib, so slight, looking worn out from her journey,
and gaze at the world and at us in dubious willingness.

The Ordeal

When our son gets braces, the next day
he gets poison ivy—his mouth is like a catch
a retriever carries back in its jaws,
and then they start to form, the welts
on his chin, ears, throat. Each hour,
gluey bubbles rise to the surface
and break, a soft fountain slowly
pours from his ear-lobe, his body weeps
from its thousand eyes. He sits steadily
facing the television, watching what's inside it
from within the scored and fluted hive
of his head. He has gone through depression, through
despair, through worry, past scratching, he has entered
a calm state, I look at him down along a
slant, the tiny world playing rapidly and
glossily on his eyeballs—and there, on his upper
lip, through the facial down, through one bead
of a weal of poison ivy, above
a tooth being slowly torn loose in its socket, a
single, thick, white whisker
curves out into the air.

The Lady Bug

The day our daughter gets into college
a lady bug flies straight toward our bed
and lands on my pillow. Head down,
it trudges along rapidly, its
furled wings sticking out the back
from under the red shell. I wet
my thumb in tea, it mounts the thumb,
I hold still, as when first nursing,
breathing evenly. After
a while it drops to the pillowcase
and noses like a scenter. I touch some tea
to the taut percale and the lady bug
kneels in cow's milk and tannic acid, then a
joint buckles and it's lying on its rim
lapping souchong. I fetch a plate
and a leaf, wistful to build it a cage,
raise it to reproductive age
and then raise its babies. But it draws back,
lifting its feet up sharply from the icy
floral porcelain. Then I remember
it's a carnivore, I get the swatter
and go hunting for it, stun a fly, half-
crush it and set it down. The lady bug
rears up, fondles the wings,
rubs the fondle up its forearms, then
takes a tour of the whole creature
three times its size, licks the leg-barbs,
noses into the anus, treads across the
bulbs of the eyes. I lean over, and remember
the first days of our daughter's life
when I bent double over her cradle

as she slept, my tears odd, wild,
tropical spots on the cot-sheet,
I swore to her I'd raise her until in her strength she could leave me.

The Bonding

He comes home from the braces doctor
scratchy-brilliant, a toy prison
inserted in his mouth—he looks as if
he's eating a little toaster. His sister
asks him where it hurts, she studies him.
The next week, she comes home
grinning a similar grin, her brother
parts her lips with his fingers to see
if her tie-wires are the same, her stainless steel
ligatures. They smile at each other,
then they try to end the smiles,
pulling their upper lips with their fingers
over the shining appliances.
The outlines of their faces have changed,
their mouths swelled out to contain the bristling
hardware set, and when they talk
there's a spray in the air between them, the hiss
of an orthodontial lisp—in the back
seat of the car, that night, it hangs
like mist at the base of a huge falls
while they chatter as if we were not there,
they have entered a new tribe together
which speaks its own sibilant language.
Slowly they drift into silence, and when
we stop to change drivers I turn and look—
heads flung back, they sleep, their mouths
open in pain and amazement.

High School Senior

For seventeen years, her breath in the house
at night, puff, puff, like summer
cumulus above her bed,
and her scalp smelling of apricots
—this being who had formed within me,
squatted like a bright tree-frog in the dark,
like an eohippus she had come out of history
slowly, through me, into the daylight,
I had the daily sight of her,
like food or air she was there, like a mother.
I say "college," but I feel as if I cannot tell
the difference between her leaving for college
and our parting forever—I try to see
this house without her, without her pure
depth of feeling, without her creek-brown
hair, her daedal hands with their tapered
fingers, her pupils dark as the mourning cloak's
wing, but I can't. Seventeen years
ago, in this room, she moved inside me,
I looked at the river, I could not imagine
my life with her. I gazed across the street,
and saw, in the icy winter sun,
a column of steam rush up away from the earth.
There are creatures whose children float away
at birth, and those who throat-feed their young
for weeks and never see them again. My daughter
is free and she is in me—no, my love
of her is in me, moving in my heart,
changing chambers, like something poured
from hand to hand, to be weighed and then reweighed.

The Pediatrician Retires

This is the archway where I stood, next to the
panel of frosted glass, when they told me
there was a chance it could be epilepsy, and
almost before my heart sank
I felt a fresh layer of something fold
over my will and wrap it, in an instant,
as if the body takes care of the parent
who takes care of the child. This is the door
we came through each week while the symptoms slowly
faded. That is the fruit-scale where she
weighed him, and his arms flew to the sides
in an infant Moro. And there are the chairs
where one sits with the infectious ones,
the three-year-olds calmly struggling for air, not
listless or scared, steady workers,
pulling breath through the constricted passage,
Yes, she says, *it's bronchial pneumonia
and asthma, the same as last month*, the parent's
heart suddenly stronger, like a muscle
the weight-lifter has worked. There is the room
where she took his blood and he watched the vial fill, he went
greener, and greener, and fainted, and she said,
*Next time don't be brave, next time
shout!* And here is the chair where I sat and she
said *If the nerve is dead, he will lose only
partial use of the hand, and it's
the left hand—he's right-handed, isn't he?*,
the girding, the triple binding of the heart.
This is the room where I sat, worried,
and opened the magazine, and saw
the war in Asia, a very young soldier

hanged by the neck—still a boy, almost,
not much older than the oldest children
in the waiting room. Suddenly its walls seemed
not quite real, as if we all
were in some large place together.
This is where I learned what I know,
the body university—
at graduation, we would cry, and throw
our ceiling-at-four-a.m. hats high in the air,
but I think that until the end of our life we are here.

Part 4

This Hour

We could never really say what it is like,
this hour of drinking wine together
on a hot summer night, in the living room
with the windows open, in our underwear,
my pants with pale-gold gibbon monkeys on them
gleaming in the heat. We talk about our son
disappearing between the pine boughs,
we could not tell what was chrysalis or
bough and what was him. The wine
is powerful, each mouthful holds
for a moment its amber agate shape,
I think of the sweat I sipped from my father's
forehead the hour before his death. We talk about
those last days—that I was waiting for him to die.
You are lying on the couch, your underpants
a luminous white, your hand resting
relaxed, alongside your penis,
we talk about your father's illness,
your nipple like a pure circle of
something risen to the surface of your chest.
Even if we wanted to,
we could not describe it,
the end of the second glass when I sometimes
weep and you start to get sleepy—I love
to drink and cry with you, and end up
sobbing to a sleeping man, your
long body filling the couch and
draped slightly over the ends, the
untrained soft singing of your snore, it cannot be given.
Yes, we know we will make love, but we're
not getting ready to make love,

nor are we getting over making love,
love is simply our element,
it is the summer night, we are in it.

His Father's Cadaver

The old man had always wanted
to end up there, on the chrome table,
the Medical School Dissection Room
on that island in the North Atlantic
his heaven. So his only child signed the papers—
son, M.D. He knew that the students
would start with a butterfly incision,
cutting the body down the center, lifting
the skin of the chest and the abdomen up
and out to the sides. He had heard the high
neutral scream of the bone-saw, he knew
they would pry back the ribs to get at the heart.
He knew the pattern they followed, he had done it himself—
chest, abdomen, head, hands,
feet. They would stand there, the medical students,
day after day, around his father,
one doing a knee, one
the bowels, the scalp, the eye, the face.
This is what his father had wanted,
to throw himself bodily into the hospital like a
roe-fish thrown back, to enter his students
directly, as knowledge—
so the wreckage could be seen as good, even
his chest, which might look gnawed, his jaws
shining through as they removed his lips,
even the pool of slurry like the fish factory—
and every week his son had some idea
where they might be, as those at home
will chart the route of Arctic explorers,
the pins on the map moving in
through the cold toward the center. He knew if it got

too crowded at the gurney, someone would take
the brain over to another table
to separate it, into its parts, like a
god his father would move, piece
by piece, out into the world. At night,
they would cover everything with plastic bags,
the veins and arteries lying fanned out
across the back of the hand—by day they were
murmuring Latin, memorizing the old man.
For six months, from two thousand miles,
the son follows it, with occasional horror,
with respect, the long dismantling
of that man who used to grease him down
and lower him into the Bay of Fundy
to check on his wave machine, which he hoped
would harness the power of the sea, that man who had
delivered him, his palm waiting under
the head when it came forth, trusting
himself, best, to touch, first,
the mortal boy they had made.

West

The hair I pull, out of my comb,
drifts off, from the rail of the porch.
It is curled on itself, it folds, kneels,
bows and buckles over onto the earth.
This is the soil I came from, sour
tang of resin and baked dust.
I saw my father's ashes down
into the dirt, except for the portion I
put on my tongue like the Host and swallowed and ate.
I have always wanted to cross over
into the other person, draw the
other person over into me.
Fast are the naked palms to the breasts
from behind, at the porch rail, fast
is a look. Slow is knowing where I come from,
who I might be, like a dream of matter
looking for spirit. Now the hair
rises on an updraft, wobbling, reddish,
in a half-circle, it wavers higher—
the jelly head of the follicle
has the tail of the hair in its mouth, it rolls back
up, toward me, through the morning, as if
someone, somewhere, were saying, to me, we are one now.

Lifelong

When I think of your tail-bone, the tart sweetness
of its skin, and, in the bone, the marrow,
the packed, quartz crystals of Northern
rock, glimmering, after the glacier,
I think of how we travel, easily,
into each other, it is where we go
at night. There is ocean, sky, granite,
there is your father, dead, curled on his side,
mouth open, lips cracked,
and my father, his jaw at the same grim
angle of a salt-cod, and their seed
is there, too. I do not know
where the mothers are, maybe the mothers
are elsewhere, and I can be the only
woman for a while, and love the entire
human in the man. Smooth and planished
under the stars, your tailbone at night almost
phosphors—I touch it as we dive, through a dark
like a cold and unlighted Atlantic, bands
of seed rich as krill in the water,
down to the floor of our life together, and the
door that opens in that floor, and stands open, and we dive.

Full Summer

I paused, and paused, over your body,
to feel the current of desire pull
and pull through me. Our hair was still wet,
mine like knotted wrack, it fell
across you as I paused, a soaked coil
around your glans. When one of your hairs
dried, it lifted like a bare nerve.
On the beach, above us, a cloud had appeared
in the clear air, a clockwise loop
coming in out of nothing, now the skin of your scrotum
moved like a live being, an animal,
I began to lick you, the foreskin lightly
stuck in one spot, like a petal, I love
to free it—just so—in joy,
and to sip from the little crying lips
at the tip. Then there was no more pausing,
nor was this the taker,
some new one came
and sucked, and up from where I had been hiding I was
drawn in a heavy spiral out of matter
over into another world
I had thought I would have to die to reach.

Last Night

The next day, I am almost afraid.
Love? It was more like dragonflies
in the sun, 100 degrees at noon,
the ends of their abdomens stuck together, I
close my eyes when I remember. I hardly
knew myself, like something twisting and
twisting out of a chrysalis,
enormous, without language, all
head, all shut eyes, and the humming
like madness, the way they writhe away,
and do not leave, back, back,
away, back. Did I know you? No kiss,
no tenderness—more like killing, death-grip
holding to life, genitals
like violent hands clasped tight
barely moving, more like being closed
in a great jaw and eaten, and the screaming
I groan to remember it, and when we started
to die, then I refuse to remember,
the way a drunkard forgets. After,
you held my hands extremely hard as my
body moved in shudders like the ferry when its
axle is loosed past engagement, you kept me
sealed exactly against you, our hairlines
wet as the arc of a gateway after
a cloudburst, you secured me in your arms till I slept—
that was love, and we woke in the morning
clasped, fragrant, buoyant, that was
the morning after love.

Am and Am Not

When I am tilted forward, brushing my teeth,
I glance down. We do not know
ourselves. My cunt, like a hand, stroked him,
such subtle, intricate movement. Central
inside me this one I am and am not,
not only like a palm, more like a snake's
reticulated body, rings of muscle—
like the penis outside-in, its twin.
Who is it? I lean against the sink, mouth open
and burning with Colgate, nixie palate
scoured with pond-mint; is it my soul
in there, elastic as an early creature
gone out on its own again, is it
my soul's throat? Its rings ripple
in waves, as if it swallows, but what it
swallows stays, and grows, and grows,
we become one being, whom we hardly know,
whom we know better than we know anyone
else. And in the morning I look down. Who? What has—
what?! Seeing just the skin of the belly—
she is asleep in there, the soul, vertical
undulant one, she is dancing upright in her dream.

True Love

In the middle of the night, when we get up
after making love, we look at each other in
complete friendship, we know so fully
what the other has been doing. Bound to each other
like mountaineers coming down from a mountain,
bound with the tie of the delivery-room,
we wander down the hall to the bathroom, I can
hardly walk, I wobble through the granular
shadowless air, I know where you are
with my eyes closed, we are bound to each other
with huge invisible threads, our sexes
muted, exhausted, crushed, the whole
body a sex—surely this
is the most blessed time of my life,
our children asleep in their beds, each fate
like a vein of abiding mineral
not discovered yet. I sit
on the toilet in the night, you are somewhere in the room,
I open the window and snow has fallen in a
steep drift, against the pane, I
look up, into it,
a wall of cold crystals, silent
and glistening, I quietly call to you
and you come and hold my hand and I say
I cannot see beyond it. I cannot see beyond it.

A NOTE ABOUT THE AUTHOR

Sharon Olds was born in 1942, in San Francisco, and educated at Stanford University and Columbia University. Her first book, *Satan Says* (1980), received the inaugural San Francisco Poetry Center Award. Her second, *The Dead and the Living*, was both the Lamont Poetry Selection for 1983 and winner of the National Book Critics Circle Award. *The Father* was shortlisted for the T. S. Eliot Prize in England. She teaches poetry workshops in the Graduate Creative Writing Program at New York University and helps run the N.Y.U. workshop program at Goldwater Hospital on Roosevelt Island in New York.

A NOTE ON THE TYPE

This book was set in Janson, a typeface long thought to have been made by the Dutchman Anton Janson, who was a practicing type-founder in Leipzig during the years 1668–1687. However, it has been conclusively demonstrated that these types are actually the work of Nicholas Kis (1650–1702), a Hungarian, who most probably learned his trade from the master Dutch typefounder Dirk Voskens. The type is an excellent example of the influential and sturdy Dutch types that prevailed in England up to the time William Caslon (1692–1766) developed his own incomparable designs from them.

Composed by North Market Street Graphics,
Lancaster, Pennsylvania

Printed at The Stinehour Press,
Lunenburg, Vermont

Bound at The Book Press,
Brattleboro, Vermont

Based on a design by Judith Henry